The Light That Brought Me Through

By Debra Hutcherson

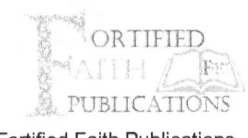

Fortified Faith Publications

Copyright © 2016 by Debra Hutcherson

All rights reserved. This book or any portion thereof may not be reproduced or used in any manner whatsoever without the express written permission of the publisher except for the use of brief quotations in a book review. All rights reserved. No part of this publication may be reproduced, distributed, or transmitted in any form or by any means, including photocopying, recording, or other electronic or mechanical methods, without the prior written permission of the publisher, except in the case of brief quotations embodied in critical reviews and certain other noncommercial uses permitted by copyright law.

Printed in the United States of America

First Edition, 2019

ISBN 978-1-7338619-0-8

Fortified Publications
20 N. 78th St.
Belleville, IL 62223

Book formatting and edited by Tamara Anderson in Belleville, IL.
Cover design by Anointed Graphics © 2019. All rights reserved.

Acknowledgements

To God be the Glory

Thank you to all the people who have supported me throughout my life and now as I write this book. Thank you to my four loving children; my daughter Monica and my sons William, Diamond, and Aaron. To my six dear grandchildren who always bring me joy and happiness. Thank you to my cousin Faye, my former Pastor Reginald Rogers, Sr., and his dedicated wife, Vickie, as well as my eight wonderful siblings. And a special Thank You to my devoted and caring husband and mentor, Tyrone; I'm grateful to you all for your love and support. "I shall not die, but live, declare the works of the LORD," Psalm 118:17.

Table of Contents

Prologue

Chapter 1
- Dickson Street 1

Chapter 2
- The First Sorrow on Dickson Street..................9

Chapter 3
- The Dark Side of Dickson Street 15

Chapter 4
- The Fear on Dayton Street 27

Chapter 5
- Secure on Athlone Street 35

Chapter 6
- The Prayers on Marcus Street........................41

Chapter 7
- Reunited But Still Many Troubles 59

Chapter 8
- Life Begins With Jim on Emerson St. 65

Chapter 9
- Life Continues on Alcott St. 73

Chapter 10
    Life with Jim on Many Streets..........................79
Chapter 11
    Life Changes on Poplar St. Bridge 85
Chapter 12
    Help on Union Street 95
Chapter 13
    Peace in a Shelter 99

Prologue

The Accident

One evening, two days before the Fourth of July of 2001, my ex-husband and I went to get some fireworks for our son and grandchildren to shoot off for the holiday. There was an eight-year age difference between my ex-husband, Jim, and I. Life with him over the years went from bad to worse. He had become an alcoholic, very controlling, and abusive. Jim abused me physically and mentally. Living with him became more and more intolerable because he was selfish and his whole life revolved around gambling in casinos and befriending undesirable people.

As the years passed, his manipulative ways continued to worsen. I even got tired of Jim's drunkenness and not having the peace of mind that God intended for me according to Philippians 4:7, "And the peace of God, which passeth all understanding, shall keep your hearts and minds through Jesus Christ."

The store where we went to purchase the fireworks from was located in Southern Illinois and we lived in St. Louis, MO. After purchasing the fireworks, while on the highway returning home, a speeding car suddenly ran into us and our car hit the retaining wall on the Martin Luther King Bridge.

One week before the accident I prayed for God to help me in my walk with Him. I asked Him to make a change in my life. I was tired of being spiritual only on Sundays and living worldly Monday through Saturday. God heard my prayer and told me what to do; He instructed me to pray every day and read His word once a day after coming home from work.

I believe because I was obedient to God's instructions, my life was spared. I am thankful to the doctors and nurses that treated me while I was in their care at St. Mary's Hospital. I was later transferred to Barnes Jewish Hospital in the city of St. Louis, MO. I also thankful to the doctors at Barnes Jewish Hospital.

While I was a patient at Barnes Hospital I saw a beam of light and a voice spoke to me through the foggy cloud. While I can't remember the words exactly now, the voice was deep but beautiful. I began screaming and yelling, "Thank you Jesus, thank you Jesus", not fully aware of where I was nor of all the detail to what had taken place.

This is my story

Thy word is a lamp unto my feet, and a light unto my path.

Psalm 119:105

Chapter 1
Dickson Street

Growing up as a child was very difficult for me. I can remember things from a very young age that happened in my family that will always stick in my heart and mind. One of my earliest memories is of my father, mother, brothers, sisters, and I all living in a three-multifunctional-room house on "struggling" Dickson St. The reason I call it "struggling" Dickson St. is because of the hard times in life we had at that address. One of the main reasons we struggled on Dickson St. is due to the death of my mother. After her passing my father was unable to provide the necessities we needed, such as toiletries, food, clothing, and utilities.

My blessed birth made me the seventh child of my parents; three boys and four girls. Immediately after me, my mother had a baby that was stillborn. He was named, Billy, and was given a birth certificate. I wonder what he would have been like if God had allowed him to live. Had he lived, my parents would have had ten children total, but nine youngsters were more than enough for Daddy and Mama.

God has allowed me to remember some of my childhood starting at the early age of one-year-old. Some of the incidents that took place have remained in my heart. While certain ones may seem less significant than others, they are all important to me because having suffered brain damage following the car accident with memory loss, I am just blessed to have some remembrances from my youth. I do recall that we received direct sunlight only in the kitchen, which caused the whole house to seem slightly gloomy, however, the apartment was always clean and active with children's laughter, cries and shouts.

One of my earliest memories happened one summer day in 1960. We had to enter our apartment from the back hallway. Daddy and Mama slept in the middle room while the girls slept in the large living room on a sofa sleeper. The three boys had to sleep on a rollaway bed in the kitchen, which they had to put away every morning to make room for meals. I was the youngest of seven at that time. This allowed me to sleep in the protective custodial arms of Mama. We were always together, which was critically important during the bad times.

I can barely recall the moment; Mama was lying in her bed trying to take a nap in her bedroom, that was right off the kitchen. Mama had her bed where she could see the screen door. The headboard sat against the wall going toward the hallway and the foot of the bed sat in the middle of the floor. To get from the living room to the kitchen you had to go around the bed. The sun was shining bright through the screen door as I was lying next to Mama. I could hear my brothers and sisters laughing and talking while playing in the backyard. I began moving all over that one spot, struggling to peek over the end of the bed as I desperately wanted to go out and play with my siblings. But Mama did not trust them to keep a steady eye on me.

Mama was getting sleepier and sleepier and as I went to pop my head up once more, she said to me, "Lay down girl and go to sleep." Just then Norma Jean burst into the kitchen, with the screen door slamming behind her screaming and crying. "What is wrong with you girl?" Mama asked. Between the sobbing and pain, she told Mama that Melvin hit her in the eye with a rock. Mama was used to Melvin picking on Norma Jean, teasing, and aggravating her knowing that she would come running and beg Mama to tell Melvin to leave her alone. Mama didn't get up from her bed to inspect Norma Jean's eye because she could see from where she was lying that she was not bleeding. Mama called for Norma Jean to come to the bed so she could carefully examine her eye. Mama blew in it then finding nothing, dismissively yelled at Melvin to stop throwing rocks. I can remember her saying "Stop throwing rocks before you put someone's eye out boy!" All of the excitement was over, and Mama laid me down for the last time. I laid there for a while still trying to peek over the end of the bed. I would raise up a little and Mama would feel me moving and say lay down in a very sleepy voice. As soon as I thought she was asleep, amused, I peeked over the foot of the bed and an odd movement caught my eye. I remember fragmented clips of what came next.

What appeared to be the head of a very small man was moving methodically at the foot of Daddy and Mama's bed. Being a very small child, I chuckled at what I was looking at. I peeked over the foot of the bed again, I saw a little man this time, and he was going up and down as he was playing with me. The man was very short with thick dark hair, heavy eyebrows, burly mustache, and beard; he reminded me of a troll as he was going up and down. I began to smile. The memory of the troll has oddly stuck with me throughout the years. Even at a young age, I knew enough of the family code to keep such observations to myself. I felt no one would believe me even as I grew older. It's an old saying when babies are laughing and there is nothing there, they are playing with angels. You never know what they may be seeing that makes them laugh.

Another memory that has stuck in my heart is when Mama took me on a trip without the other children. On this day, Mama got me dressed to go with her to my aunt's house. Mama had me looking so pretty in my pink dress with a matching pink bonnet on my head. Mama had on a red dress and a scarf that had big black tassels hanging from the bottom of it and in the middle of the scarf was a big black button. The house on Dickson St. had several steps.

There were three immediately leaving out of the house then there was a small walk way and about five more steps before you got to the sidewalk. While waiting on the cab that she ordered, Mama and I sat on the top set of steps. I continued to play with the button on Mama's dress until all of a sudden, I heard a horn blow. I turned around to look and saw a red taxi cab. Mama sat me on her lap and the cab driver began to drive off.

    During the ride in the taxi cab, which seemed to take a long time, I looked out of the window and saw lots of wooded areas. Many years later I learned, from my older sister Betty, that my aunt lived in a small township in St. Louis, MO called Kinloch. This community had a small population with very few houses. The cab driver stopped the cab and opened the door allowing Mama to get out of the taxi. Although I don't remember if my aunt had steps on her house are not, I do remember the house seemed to be a straight through sort of house; where when you go in the front door you can see the backyard of the house. This type of house was generally called a "shotgun house". Mama took me in her arms and we walked in the front door; she began talking to her sisters. It amazes me that I can remember these details like it was yesterday, but I don't recall anything after that. Not how long we stayed, how we got home or why we really were there to begin with.

The next occurrence I can elicit took place when I was between two and three years old; I just know that I was still a toddler. I recall being in the kitchen with Daddy while he was cooking something, I don't remember what it was but it smelled good. There was a knock at the front door; Mama answered it and began talking to my two aunts as they were coming in the front door. They were talking very loudly and my other siblings may have been outside or watching television. I came into the living room where Mama was along with my two aunts as they were all sitting on the couch. As Mama was entertaining them in conversation, I eased my little self over to the coffee table. I began to play with her trinkets that she had on the table, even though Mama did not allow any of her children nor anyone else to bother them. I was standing there looking at all the pretty decorations on the table, though there was not many, there was just enough to catch my little eyes. Thinking I could get away with something because we had visitors, I decided to touch her decorations. Boy, what did I do that for knowing that she was going to tap my little hand. I tried touching them again. This time she said, "No, No!" Being a toddler, I thought I could try it again; this time she changed "No, no!" to "What did I tell you?" along with a spank on the hand. I cried aloud and after that I don't remember bothering anything else on her coffee table. After I calmed down, she picked me up and sat me on her lap and continued her conversation once again with her guests.

As time passed Mama had another baby; a boy named Carl. This was her ninth child, including Billy. I can't remember my parents bringing Carl home, but I do remember him crawling throughout the house. Carl was a very quiet baby, he kept a bottle hanging from his mouth and sat quietly off to himself. There's not much more I can remember from Carl being a baby; the memories resume when he began to walk. Daddy and Mama remained at this address on Dickson St. for a while longer. They ended up having their tenth baby, when I was about three years old, Danny.

We lived there at that same house until I was four years old. During those times children were not allowed to hang around when adults were talking so we did not hear a lot of what the grown-ups were talking about nor did we ask them questions. So, when Mama became ill, around the time Danny turned four months old, we had no idea of what was going on. It was during this time that I could not resort to Mama to carry my burdens nor did I understand why Mama had to go and leave me. This was the beginning of the great first sorrow on Dickson St.

Chapter 2

The First Sorrow on Dickson Street

Throughout my very early years, Mama was always close to me and I was always under her protective guardianship. She was a deity of strength and stoicism that solved all the great sibling conflicts and worked side by side with Daddy to make sure we had what we needed. Mama was glorious and impervious to anything that would take down other people. In her presence, I never had to fully rely on myself for strength and protection; it was natural to feel that she would remain my shield and armor forever.

The day Mama was removed from the house was very devastating for me. I can remember Mama lying in her bed with the new baby, Danny, laying in her arms, my sisters and brothers sitting on the couch. My little brother Carl was sitting on my older brother Chucky's lap with his bottle hanging from his mouth. In the 60's, children were not privy to adult business or matters and if they did find out information, it was kept amongst themselves. They didn't let grown-ups know that they knew what was going on.

I distinctly remember, on that day, seeing two white men coming into our house; which was an extraordinarily unusual occurrence. Daddy talked to the men momentarily and then they turned and proceeded to go out the front door. I ran to the living room, stood on the couch in front of the window to see where the men were going. I saw a black and white ambulance parked in front of the house. While peeking out the window the two men opened the back door of the ambulance and pulled out a long flat, skinny bed with four wheels, two on the back and two on the front. The bed had draping white sheets and big straps and buckles. As the two men were coming up the stairs, I jumped down from the couch and hurried back into Mama's room.

    I walked towards the end of the bed until Daddy said "Move out the way! Get over there and sit down," with a deep, husky, firm voice. Just the right tone for me to sit my little self-down with my sisters and brothers. Daddy picked up Danny from Mama's embrace and handed him to my oldest sister Betty. The two men delicately lifted Mama from where she quietly laid, onto the long and narrow bed. The men silently strapped the belt buckles to her waist, arms and ankles. They made sure Mama was safe and secure on the long skinny narrow bed. Then the strangers began solemnly walking with the bed holding the bottom as they went out of the front door. Daddy was walking glumly behind the men leaving our house, going down toward the ambulance. I started to feel something was not right. I rushed back to the couch. This time, my siblings and I hurried to look out of the window because Daddy blurted, "I'll be right back." Daddy got into the back of the ambulance with one man. The other man got into the front of the ambulance and they sped off with the sirens blaring. My sisters and brothers began to talk amongst themselves about what they saw; I still did not understand all the events that had just taken place. I do know that was the last time I saw Mama.

I can remember my siblings and I were left alone for what seemed like forever. When Daddy came home that night, we were moving aimlessly all over the house. It seemed pointless to watch television. This particular night, when Daddy came home, he entered through the back door. We heard a loud noise coming from the kitchen door. Daddy had flung the door open, stumbling onto the kitchen floor. With a loud thud and a shrieking cry, he laid on the floor as if he had been attacked. My older siblings and I dared not to come too close to Daddy. We were frightened and curious about his strange behaviors. We could only look with quiet terror but could not search for answers about his actions. We couldn't see any marks or bruises, yet the hurt he displayed was extremely visible.

Daddy laid there sobbing as if someone had taken his heart out and crushed it. My older brother Chucky asked Daddy what was wrong? Daddy got up from the floor and told us to sit down. "I have something to tell y'all," he said. "Y'all Mama just died," with hurt still in his eyes. The next day my siblings did not go to school. People from the little church that was located at 2922 Dickson St. began to come over to our house. The word traveled extremely fast that Mama had died. I didn't know what to think other than Mama was not coming back home to me.

One night two ladies came over to help Daddy get us younger children dressed for the funeral. These ladies came from the same little church as the others did. I stood and starred as if I saw something phenomenal. One lady had a pretty and pleasant face with a beautiful smile; in contrast, the other lady looked uptight and fussy. After putting on my clothes, the fussy lady began to undo my braids. She yanked my hair and combed it very harshly. She did not appreciate me squirming nor my cries from the pain. This strange lady made me feel afraid and long for Mama. In a mean and unsympathetic voice, she told me to shut up. She said this quietly so no one else could hear her other than me. After getting us all dressed, the two ladies took some of us out of the house and directed us to the open door of a long black car. Daddy and the rest of the children joined us. Once all of us was in, the driver drove off.

As I reminiscence back, the long black car stopped at a small building. There were other cars parking as we pulled up. There were people getting out of their cars and heading for the entrance of the funeral parlor. The casket sat in front of a wall and right next to a podium near the corner was a man speaking loudly so that everyone in the small room could see and hear him. I sat on Daddy's lap and two of my siblings held Carl and Danny on their laps. For the viewing of Mama's body, I was walked along side of Daddy holding his hand. Uncle Sam came up from behind and picked me up under my arms so that I could get a peek at Mama's body. That's exactly what it was, a peek, and back to the floor I returned.

    The next morning, Daddy got us dressed to go to the burial site. Everyone loaded in their cars respectively. The hearse, carrying Mama's casket, was the first car in the line and immediately following was the long black car with us in it. All other cars followed behind. Once at the burial site, everyone got out of their cars again and the man that spoke at the funeral started talking once more. That was the last time I remember seeing Mama. A few days passed and I can remember there was a knock at the front door. I came from the living room to look and there stood two of my Daddy's sisters and one of my Daddy's aunt. She stood there looking with a pleasant smile on her face and my Daddy's sisters started talking to Daddy for a moment. Before Daddy knew it, they all were just taking Mama's things without his permission. Mama had lots of beautiful clothes, jewelry, shoes, and coats. They were packing Mama's things as if they were at a clothing store catching a sale. Within just a short time, they had her stuff and were gone except for my great-aunt. The only thing they left was a mink stole with two fox heads on each side; they should have taken that one because Melvin liked to scare us smaller kids with it.

    After the death of Mama, over time, things began to get worse. Daddy tried hard to keep his job at the Chase Park Plaza Hotel, but there was no one to look after Carl, Danny, and I. He started to let my older brothers and sisters take turns staying home from school to watch us. It was not long until Daddy had to get a different job in an attempt to make enough money to pay the bills. This new job kept him away from home a lot. This job did not pay enough money for rent, electricity, and gas. We were without electricity and gas and was forced to use oil lamps at night. There was no more TV watching and Daddy had to cook on an oil stove. This is when the dark side of Dickson St. began.

Chapter 3

The Dark Side of Dickson Street

With Daddy's new job, we never knew when he would return home. It could have been anywhere from one to three days between his stays. All I do know is whenever Daddy returned home I was glad to see him. The time came when my older siblings were getting a little out of hand. There was no one there to discipline them. But thank God for our neighbors that stayed on each side of us; they would keep an eye on us while Daddy was at work. They would instruct my older siblings on when to go inside at night and tell them to stay in the front yard to keep a watchful eye. During the early 60's when I was growing up, the city of St. Louis did not allow juveniles under a certain age hanging outside or walking the streets at night. The curfew laws then stated if you were not in front of your house after a certain time the police would take you down and give your parents a ticket.

Things were never the same on Dickson St. once Mama was gone. Daddy had to take on the role as a father and mother, coming home cooking, washing, and making sure his children were taken care of. Daddy began getting weaker and weaker trying to keep us all together letting no one come in and separate him from his children. This one specific day three of my aunts came over to help knowing that Daddy was having a hard time trying to take care of nine children. One of the aunts was my Daddy's sister, another was his Aunt and the last was his sister-in-law. While I stood listening to Daddy having a conversation with them, his sister-in-law stated that she wanted to take Debbie with her. Daddy looked at her with such a strange look on his face and he began saying to them that none of his kids were going anywhere.

It was hard to see Daddy leave to go back to work because I didn't know when I would see him again. There would be days Norma Jean, Carl and I would sit out on the front steps of the house and see Daddy coming down the block. We would shout with joy "Here comes Daddy", and run to meet him knowing that he was coming to tend to our needs; food, clean clothes and most of all love. I would grab hold to his leg, Norma Jean, would grab hold to the other leg and Carl would be picked up by Daddy. He played with us all the way from the middle of the block to the house. There would be some days he would get out of a car catching a ride home because he had bags and boxes of food. We were still glad to see him. Norma Jean would let the others know here comes Daddy and when Chucky, Melvin and Bernice heard that they scrabbled around trying to straighten up the house so Daddy wouldn't have much to do while at home.

One day while Daddy was gone there was a fire at the house. My siblings were getting dressed for school when Chucky said he smelt smoke. Norma Jean just happened to look up and yelled out. She pointed to the two sliding doors between the living room and the bedroom. There were very small sparks of fire was dropping between the two doors. Chucky being the oldest would see that everything went well stepping into the shoes of Daddy, in his absence, ordered everyone out of the house. We all made it out safely and one of the neighbors called the fire department.

Daddy came home immediately once he received the news. There was no place for us to go at that time so we all went back into the smoke damaged house. The fire department arrived just in time and nothing major was destroyed. The only thing that was messed up was some smoke damage to the walls and around the windows. Daddy had Betty, Chucky, Melvin and Bernice helping him to clean and fix up what the firefighters trampled over.

It seemed as though we saw less of Daddy. However, he always made sure he would make it home so that we could have a blessed and beautiful holiday. Chucky's birthday is on the fourth of July, so Daddy came home on the third with boxes and bags of all kinds of goodies such as food, watermelons, clothes, and shoes for us. Not only that, he had fireworks; some for my older siblings to play with and some sparklers for Melvin, Bernice, Norma Jean and I Unfortunately, Carl and Danny could only watch and see how pretty the fireworks were. While Daddy was cooking barbecue in the backyard, us kids were in the front playing with the fireworks. Danny and Carl sat on the top set of steps watching while I stood at the top of the second set of steps listening to the pops from the firecrackers.

Chucky liked to hold the fireworks in his hand while lighting them. He sat on the first set of steps between Carl and Danny and me. He lit a firecracker and shouted for me to move out the way but by me standing with my back turned to Chucky, I couldn't move fast enough. It was too late, the firecracker hit me in the back. The belly top outfit I was wearing allowed the firecracker to physically touch my back and burn me. I began yelling and screaming wanting the pain to stop. I ran in the house to Daddy. He began telling Chucky and my other siblings to be careful while popping the fireworks. There wasn't a lot of damage done to my back. Daddy rubbed some kind of ointment on it, and I was back outside. Later that night, Daddy went back to his work place, as usual, down at the Market Place.

As time went on, some of my siblings began to rebel like my older brother Willie. He started staying out all hours of the night and having his friend Leroy hang around. Daddy didn't mind Leroy coming over as long as Willie was at home and not wondering around in the streets or at someone else's house. Daddy would sometimes bring gifts home for the younger children. One time he bought home two small rocking chairs for Norm Jean and I to have around the house and share with Bernice and Carl. Willie came walking in the door one afternoon making the announcement that he had just gotten married, at the age of seventeen, not expecting Daddy to be home. He knew Daddy wanted us to go to school, get our education and then get married.

Daddy was very angry about Willie making such a drastic decision like marriage on his own without his permission. He was so upset to the point where he was not thinking, grabbed Norma Jean's rocking chair and hit Willie with it. I have never seen that side of him before. Daddy asked him why did he do that. Willie didn't say anything. Before we knew it, Daddy swung the rocking chair again hitting Willie with it and breaking the little chair across his head. We knew that if our parents asked us a question, we better had answered them. Breaking Norma Jean's chair didn't bother me until Daddy picked up my chair and broke it hitting Willie once more. God was with Willie during this altercation because there was not one mark or bruise on him. After this confrontation, Willie began coming and going when he pleased giving Daddy a very hard time.

My older sister Betty also began to do things that Daddy would not approve of. While living on Dickson

St., we had several upstairs neighbors after the landlord moved out. One set of neighbors had a family with teenagers. Betty and one of the boys, Chester, found themselves liking each other. Daddy was not going for such a thing, especially Betty having a boyfriend, which was her very first one. But Daddy had to work long hours at the Market Place and there was no one to keep them apart. This family didn't live there very long. Shortly after they left another family relocated here from Mississippi. The new family had a lot of children and teenagers. Betty, not having parental guidance, began liking and listening to the boy upstairs named Jack. Jack was not the type of boy my Daddy was pleased with. He did not want the same thing to happen to Betty that happened to Willie, running off and getting married at an early age.

It wasn't too long after this family moved in that we moved out. Daddy was not able to get enough money to catch up on the back rent. I don't remember exactly when we moved, but we relocated to a house in the next block. The new house had some similarities to the old house: we lived on the first floor of the house and neighbors lived above us, it was still on Dickson St., just a block over from the old house, and the boys shared a bed while the girls shared a bed. There were also differences: the way we entered the new house (we had our own entrance), this house had four rooms instead of three, and there was not a screen door attached to the kitchen door.

Moving to a new house felt different. Daddy cleaned the whole place, covered the floors with new nylon rugs, hung new curtains, and with the help of Chucky, Betty, Melvin, and Bernice put everything in its place. He cooked and made sure we were very comfortable before he went back to the Market place to work. The newness did not last long. Once again things started to go down and we started going without the necessities that were needed like gas, electricity, and clean clothes. Daddy still did the best he could by keeping us all together; he would wash our clothes by hand when he could, use oil lamps for lighting and an oil stove for cooking and heating the house.

We didn't have enough money for our household needs let alone our school needs. I was in kindergarten and needed two cents for milk money daily. It was nothing but the grace of the Lord that made a way for me to have the money that I needed. Most of the time it came from Chucky and Melvin selling soda bottles. Things became even worse when I went to first grade. Betty was the closest thing to a mama for us. Chucky, Melvin, and Bernice took care of themselves pretty good, but for us little ones we had no one, but Betty. Willie had moved out of the house by this time.

Betty, Chucky, Melvin and Bernice would take turns keeping Carl and Danny. Norma Jean and I went to school full-time. By this time not having clean clothes sometimes became a problem especially with my first-grade teacher, Mrs. Smith. She was a very unpleasant and mean lady toward me. It was protocol when the bell rang for all the children to line up by twos with the girls first and the boys last. For some reason on this day, she took the point of one of the keys from her key ring and began poking me in the head telling me to get closer in line. I believed I was as close as I could possibly be to my partner while holding hands. I was too scared to cry even though it hurt so bad. I had another incident with this same teacher. I had nothing clean to wear to school so I put on the same clothes I had worn previously. While walking into the class with my other classmates Mrs. Smith told me that she was going to get me. Once again, I became afraid of what she was going to do. She gave the other children their school work and took me inside the coat room. She held my head down close to my body, took out this skinny stick, and began whooping me with it. After about four hits I started to cry very softly so that the other children wouldn't make fun of me. Neither of these events did I tell anyone because I was a quiet, shy, and timid child.

Just like at the old house, we had gotten to know our neighbors. And just like our old neighbors, the new neighbors helped us out when we needed them. By Betty not having Mama around to teach her about the birds and bees she was rather ignorant to what sexual relationships incurred. So, when Betty started gaining weight, our neighbor, Ms. Jackson told Betty to go to the clinic. Betty thought that she was gaining the weight from eating as she had a best friend, Bessie, who was also over weight. Betty was only sixteen years old when she found out she was pregnant.

Daddy was not pleased with what Betty had done and, in fact, he was very upset with Jack, the boy that stayed upstairs in the old house. Betty had to drop out of school. To add insult to injury, we found out, from reading the paper, that Willie had gotten into some trouble with the law. He was arrested for breaking in someone's house and was found guilty. He was sentenced to five years in prison. This did not surprise Daddy in the least, but he no longer had to worry about Willie and not knowing where he was.

Betty took on the role as mama staying home seeing that Melvin, Bernice, Norma Jean, and I were off to school and staying home to look after Carl and Danny. Daddy began to stay gone and there was a lot for Betty to do while trying to take care of her baby Robert, Danny, Carl, and me. While I don't remember having a hard time at school because we didn't have a lot, I do remember coming home was very hard not knowing if we would have a meal to eat. Betty would send Bernice and Melvin to sell soda bottles so we could buy bologna and bread. On days, we could afford it everyone only got one slice of each, on days we couldn't afford it we'd just eat cookies. There were times we would run out of oil to not only light the lamps but also heat the house. It would be cold in the house during the winter.

With Daddy being gone for days at a time, Chucky somewhat took on the role as daddy. In this role, he felt like he had to keep us protected. I remember very vividly the night that he truly stepped into the protector role. Noma Jean, Bernice and I slept in the same bed, Melvin, Carl, and Danny slept in the same room, but in another bed on the opposite wall, Betty slept on the couch in the front room and Chucky slept in the kitchen on a rollaway bed. On this night, a man picked the lock and came in while we all were asleep and took Betty's record player; he then came back in to try and rape Betty who was laying on the couch. He tried to put his hand over her mouth to keep her from screaming, but she screamed anyway waking everyone up. By Chucky sleeping in the kitchen he would always keep a knife under his pillow while he slept, with the man running through the house trying to get out the back door, Chucky took his knife and threw it at the man. He missed, but our upstairs neighbor heard all the noise, got his gun out and pointed it out the back window. He shot at the man two times. The next day Betty found out that the man was her friend Bessie's uncle; he did not get shot, but was put in jail. Thank God for our neighbors.

While the Lord had neighbors, Chucky and Betty to watch over us, He had protective angels surrounding us as well. *Psalm 91:11-12, For he shall give his angels charge over thee, to keep thee in all thy ways. They shall bear thee up in their hands, lest thou dash thy foot against a stone.* One night in the absence of Daddy, I remember Betty told Melvin to check the oil in the stove to see if it was low. Melvin liked to play a lot and you never knew when he was playing or being serious. This night was no different. Melvin lit a match to see how much oil was in the stove. Everyone heard him yelling as if he were playing as usual. Bernice asked him what was wrong with him. Melvin just continued running and screaming that he burned his face. Betty yelled for Melvin to come here so she could see his face. Melvin steady yelling and crying took off running out the front door then he ran back in yelling for someone to get him some water to put on his face. Everyone did the best they could to help him. The neighbors heard all the commotion and called for an ambulance to take Melvin to the hospital. When Melvin returned home, his face was white from where the skin pilled off; he didn't look the same. However, day by day the color came back and he began looking like the old Melvin saying, "I told y'all I was burned."

    Time went on and we continued to grow. Up until this point, my Daddy had done all he knew how to do to keep us kids together and out of trouble. Don't get me wrong, we did our dirt, but our decisions were not on my Daddy. The last day on Dickson St. started out like every other one.

That morning everyone got dressed for school, including Carl and Danny; they both were now school aged. We all left for school leaving Betty and Robert home alone. Walking home from school we saw and heard fire trucks on our street, not knowing which house they were there for, but we soon saw that they were there for our house. We could not get back into this house because it had burned up to the point we had very little to salvage. Some things did not burn up like our pictures we had stored away. I thank God no one was hurt in the fire because we were all at school, Betty and Robert were somewhere else, and Daddy was at work. Daddy made it home from work and all I remember was Chucky walking Norma Jean, Carl, Danny, and I to my Aunt Cora's house around the corner on Dayton St.

Chapter 4

The Fear on Dayton Street

I was not used to spending the night away from home, so when I found out that we had to stay all night it felt different. Then we found out that we had to make Aunt Cora's six-room house home for a while because there was no place to go. Initially it felt like a vacation where there were meals every day, clean clothes, and hot water. However, things changed living with Aunt Cora. Daddy stayed away more only stopping by to see if everything was ok and to give Aunt Cora money as he had it.

I missed having fun with Melvin and Norma Jean running through the house, throwing potatoes at one another, and the laughter we shared in the back yard. We were no longer able to sit on the front listening to music, run through the gangway, or play in the dirt in the backyard. That was all gone!

Aunt Cora was the type of person that loved hard from a distance; she had very strict rules in her house. We tried not to do anything to get her upset. Betty, Bernice, and Melvin would see to it that us small children were dressed and ready for school. Soon after arriving at Aunt Cora's, Chucky graduated from high school and enlisted into the armed forces.

Aunt Cora had four children, two boys and two girls. Her oldest son did not reside at the house; just her oldest daughter along with her three small children and her youngest boy and girl. The youngest son and daughter were about the same age as Melvin and Bernice, the oldest girl was about Chucky's age. Aunt Cora was married but her husband did not live there, but he would come by from time to time to eat and sleep there.

There were all together fifteen people living in one house. The sleeping arrangements were not ideal, but Aunt Cora did the best she could. She had her oldest daughter and her three children sleeping in a small room next to the living room, in Aunt Cora's room was two twin beds; she slept in one with her daughter and Norma Jean slept in the other, her son slept on a sofa sleeper in the living room, and she put the rest of us seven in one room with only two beds near the kitchen. Carl, Danny, and I slept in one bed while Betty and her baby boy, Robert, slept in the other twin bed. Bernice and Melvin had to make pallets on the floor.

Life with Aunt Cora was like living with a stranger. I knew she was Daddy's sister, but she would show love in her own way which was nothing like Daddy. Betty would make sure we ate, rather it was food Daddy would sometimes bring for us or food cooked by Aunt Cora. We were even still able to attend the same school located around the corner which allowed us all to walk home together. When we arrived home, we would go sit in the front room and watch television for a while before doing homework. While sitting on the floor watching television and keeping warm, by the space heater Aunt Cora had sitting in her living room, we would sometimes see mice run across the floor or right by our feet. We weren't used to seeing mice at our old houses.

Mice were just the beginning of hard times for me on Dayton St. There was an attic on the third level of the house. The steps to the attic were located at the end of the hallway where our bedroom was. Once everyone would go to bed, the mice that were up front would remain up front. But when Betty would cut the light off for us to sleep there came a loud noise sounding like a bunch of people running from down the steps all at once. I couldn't help but to wake up by the sound and the noise. These were not mice, but rats, big and bold ones and they weren't scared of people.

I remember one night while hearing the rats coming from the third floor I was so scared I jumped out of the bed where Carl and Danny was and moved Betty's baby from the middle and placed him by the wall and got between Betty and her baby. The next night I still eased in her bed by keeping little Robert where he was and I would ease on the side where the wall was. I did not care as long as I was under Betty feeling safe and secure. It was so hard to sleep knowing that these rats were around scratching the box springs and getting in the bed when we were asleep.

One night as I slept I woke up to something nibbling at my ear and I felt a sting. I jumped up calling Betty softly to not make much noise, but whining and telling her my ear is bleeding. Betty got up cleaned it, but I stayed awoke until day break. This was not the only night rats climbed up in the bed with us. I would jump or move so that they would not come too far in the bed. On another night while sleeping I felt my big toe throbbing. I pulled the cover off my body, looked down at my foot, and my toe was bleeding. A rat bit the tip of my big toe. I showed Betty my toe while everyone was getting dressed for school. The bite was small and although I felt the pain it didn't hurt so badly.

The rats were not just in the bedroom; they were all over the house. One Saturday morning while waking up being thirsty I went to get a glass of water, only to see a big dead rat floating in the dishwater. After seeing what I saw I did not want any water at that time. I also remember the time Aunt Cora told Norma Jean, Carl, Danny, and me to take a bath. Betty made sure Carl and Danny took their bath together and Norma Jean decided to run her water after them and she took a bath. After everyone took their bath I walked toward the bathroom door and as I looked I saw a big rat standing on his hind legs looking straight at me as if it was not afraid.

I ran back and jumped in the bed as if I was asleep. Aunt Cora while walking toward the kitchen saw me jump in the bed and turned around. She pulled me to the bathroom and began running water to put me in the tub. I began screaming and yelling "Leave me alone. I'm going to tell my daddy!" Aunt Cora didn't know I saw a big rat by the toilet that's why I didn't take my bath. She began pulling, shoving, and hitting me with her hand saying, "Get in there and take a bath." She pulled me in the tub and began washing my body. While I was still crying and yelling, "I'm going to tell my daddy."

Not only did my aunt's house contain mice and rats, but there were also bed bugs. We had to wake up itching not knowing what was wrong until we got to seeing bumps all over our arms and legs. We would scratch so badly until we made sores from the bumps because there was nothing to put on them. The bumps left black marks over our legs and arms. This particular night while easing Robert over a little, I saw some bugs that were small and round crawling all over the wall. I took my finger and pushed one. Nothing, but blood came out. I asked Betty what was that she said bed bugs.

Daddy came home to check on us and before he could get up the steps, Danny ran to tell Daddy saying, "Daddy Aunt Cora whooped Debbie last night!" Daddy went straight to the backroom and asked Betty what happened. By Bernice witnessing the whopping she couldn't wait to tell what happened. Aunt Cora came to the back after hearing Daddy come in. She began yelling saying "Give me some money!" Daddy said, "I don't have no money!" They went back and forth before we knew it they were fighting, and she took all of our boxes of clothes and began to throw them out of the side window. Everything began flying over the gangway. The worst thing about that situation was that the friends next door that we made while living there saw us getting thrown out. I was so embarrassed.

Daddy had us picking up our things from the ground while Bernice and Melvin went to call Uncle Sam and Betty called her boyfriend Jack to come. We all went to stay with Uncle Sam. Aunt Cora did not know I was happy to leave from among the rats, but not in that way. Thank God for Uncle Sam coming to get us.

Uncle Sam had a pick-up where we all could fit in the back with our bags of clothes by the way Aunt Cora as time when on suffer for many years with a bone disease that was why she always rubbed her legs with some kind of ointment by the space heater. As time passed she was placed in a nursing home suffering until she died. While at her funeral her youngest son sat behind me while talking to someone else saying, "I wonder why God let mama suffer for so long with that muscle disease?"

I thank God for allowing Aunt Cora to help us when she did. Thank God for sending Uncle Sam for receiving us and making us feel safe and secure on Athlone St.

Chapter 5
Secure on Athlone Street

When we arrived at Uncle Sam's duplex, three of his daughters were standing on the top porch looking down at us as we stumbled out of the back of the pick-up truck with our stuff. The girls stared at us wordlessly and without smiles. They asked Uncle Sam who we were. In a very atypical but soft and gentle response, Uncle Sam looked up and answered, "They are your cousins and they are going to stay with us a little while. It's going to be all right." In an irritated, discouraging tone, "I don't want them ugly kids here," one girl pouted.

Before this day, we kids had never met. My Uncle Sam would come by every now and then to visit Daddy, his brother, but when he did, he didn't bring his children. We never traveled the distance to their house because of a lack of transportation.

Uncle Sam had an additional five children of all mixed ages which meant that there was someone for all of us to play with. He and Aunt Louise were separated at that time and all the children except the oldest, Ronald, lived with her. They would come to visit on the weekends and holidays. Knowing this information, later, helped me to understand why my one cousin felt the way she did about us staying there; she didn't want anyone coming between her and her father.

Uncle Sam opened the door to his house and everyone began going up some steps following behind him. He was a very quiet man and didn't talk a lot like Daddy, but he would show not only his children but us as well, much love. We could rely on getting hot water and plenty of food at Uncle Sam's house. The lights always came on when we flipped the switch and the flame on the gas stove constantly flickered when we turned the knob. He even had a washer and dryer. We were truly able to stand on God's word, *"But my God shall supply all your need according to his riches in glory by Christ Jesus. Philippians 4:19"*

While Uncle Sam still demanded respect as a figure of authority, he was not inclined to yelling at us or finding ways to restrict or punish us for being kids. He allowed us to feel so much at home. We could cook the food that he brought home from the packing house where he slaughtered pigs. Once we were all moved in and everyone started getting to know one another, the house was one of harmony, peace, and cleanliness.

We all had to start a new school that was located within the same block, but on the other side of the street. I was in the fourth grade during this time. Bernice tried to take Betty's place, in the mama roll, with Norma Jean, Carl, Danny, and I trying to see to it that our hair was combed and everyone had clean clothes.

Uncle Sam would bring his children home every Friday evening around the same time after work. We all looked forward to seeing them because we knew that we would have fun. I remember on hot summer Saturdays nights Uncle Sam would take us all to the market place to get peaches. We would all, except for the older children, pack up in the back of the pick-truck. After Uncle Sam would purchase the peaches he would give us all one big juicy peach to eat. There was this one special time when after eating the peaches, one of my cousins whispered to us conspiratorially, "Let's all save our seed and when we see somebody, throw our seeds at them." We all laughed and agreed with what she said. Uncle Sam drove the truck in complete ignorant bliss as we threw seeds from the back of his truck; if he knew what we had done, all of us would have gotten in so much trouble.

Uncle Sam worked long hours, leaving early before school started and not returning until way after dinner. During the week, there wasn't much for us to get into. Bernice would spend a lot of time with her boyfriend after attending to us younger children, Ronald and Melvin would fool around with Uncle Sam's tools in the basement, and us younger ones would watch a lot of television.

On the weekends, things were much different. On Saturdays Uncle Sam would leave money for each of us kids to get fifty cents. The older guys would leave the house and the rest of us would go to the local candy store, spending all our money on candy. I remember some of the kids would doing things that they knew they shouldn't have been doing such as; throwing eggs at the girl next door's window or calling the police when just for fun telling them we were alone and heard someone in the basement. My older cousin would try to keep us busy and out of trouble. She allowed us to play with the neighborhood kids when their parents were ok with it. We even had pretend talent shows. Everyone would take turns being the audience and singing.

Daddy would still come by when he was able and cook for us. He continued to make time for us on holidays. That Christmas was a special one. We had no idea that we would be receiving gifts, but Daddy surprised us with lots of toys. He had brought them by the house before Christmas and hid them in Uncle Sam's closet. Ronald was aware of this and a couple of days before Christmas he showed us our hidden gifts. Unaware that Daddy would show up on this day, we unwrapped the gifts and went down to the basement to play with our new toys. Daddy came down the steps, peeked his head in the basement, and suddenly, we stopped in total fear. We thought that we were in deep trouble for opening the gifts. Daddy was not happy with us but no one got into any serious trouble. The gifts were rewrapped and put out on Christmas Eve for us to open on Christmas Day.

As time passed, Aunt Louise and Uncle Sam decided to get back together for the sake of the children which meant that we had to move out. I thank God for Uncle Sam and Aunt Louise helping us when we needed them. When we were kicked out of Aunt Cora's place, Betty moved in with her boyfriend Jack getting a place of their own. By the time we moved out of Uncle Sam's house, I was ten years old, going into the fifth grade, and Betty and Jack had three children together. Betty agreed to allow me to move in with her and Jack. When we all left Uncle Sam's house, I lost communication with the rest of my siblings. This is when the prayers on Marcus St. , began.

Chapter 6

The Prayers on Marcus Street

When Aunt Cora put us out of her house, Betty moved in with her boyfriend Jack. They moved into a small two-story house, similar to a bungalow, with a small upstairs on a street called Fair Ground Place. Jack's niece and her children stayed upstairs which he had converted into an apartment for her. Even though we were all piled into this small house, I didn't mind because we were all together.

In the living room Jack had a bar stool that he sat on and played his guitar. He played the same song over and over every single day. He did not work. Betty had her own children to tend after so Bernice would make sure that Norma Jean, Carl, Danny, and I were taken care of. Melvin and Bernice pretty much took care of themselves. Uncle Sam made us feel welcomed, but Jack made us feel unwelcomed. He would not allow Betty to let us get what we wanted to eat out of the refrigerator. It was nothing like being at Uncle Sam's house where we could get whatever we wanted to eat without anyone saying anything about it. He would constantly complain to Betty about the food. Jack decided to put a padlock on the refrigerator. That must not have been good enough because one day when we got home from school

Jack had moved the refrigerator into their bedroom. The kitchen felt empty with just a stove and table with no refrigerator, but Betty would make sure Bernice would call Daddy so that we would have food to eat.

Daddy would come by the house to bring us what we need like food, clean clothes, and school supplies. He knew Jack was not the man to marry Betty, but there was not much he could do because she was in love with him and we had nowhere to go. Not too long after us moving in with Betty, Jack decided to move her and their children into another place on a street called Marcus. This is when my prayers begin.

Jack did not want our family staying with them anymore because of the things he was putting Betty through. He started having a lot of his friends come over hanging around and sitting in the living room. We had to stay in the small room where we slept when they came to visit. I don't remember when Betty and Jack found another place, but I do remember one evening while everyone was sitting around listening to Jack play that same song over and over on his guitar, he stopped playing for a second and began to say to Betty they were going to move. No one knew what he was talking about and we all looked shocked as if to say, "What are we going to do now and where are we going to move." We had just moved in and to move right back out was beyond us. We all wondered why Betty and Jack were moving out so fast.

Jack said boldly, "I am not taking anyone with me, but Debbie." I felt a since of relief knowing that I would have food and a place to stay, but what about Melvin, Bernice, Norma Jean, Carl, and Danny. The day came for Jack and Betty to move; one of Jack's sisters asked Betty if Norma Jean could live with her so that she could babysit her little girl in the evening while she worked. Betty said yes. So, Norma Jean felt a since of security for a little while.

Jack and Betty moved into this three-room four family duplex with their three boys and me. This is when I lost communication with my siblings. This is also when I began to wonder why me. Being separated from Melvin, Bernice, Norma Jean, Carl, and Danny felt different; I was not used to being alone without knowing where they were or could have gone to live.

By Norma Jean living with Jack's sister, she would bring her little girl and Norma Jean over to play. When Norma Jean would come over to play she would fill my ears with lies having me think she lived in a great place. She had me feeling as if she was a rich girl because she would be wearing new clothes, talked about the different places she was able to go, and the different foods she was able to eat. She knew that I couldn't eat what I wanted, Betty couldn't buy me new clothes, nor take me to those fancy places. I didn't want to hear this because I felt left out thinking the same thing was happening with Bernice, Melvin, Carl, and Danny.

At that time, I was about twelve years old and Betty enrolled me in the school around the corner. I had one of the most caring teachers. She was a very pleasant and kind lady. Living with Betty, she did not have the money to buy me things such as clothing and shoes; so, I had to go to school wearing the same thing over and over not looking my best. I really began missing Daddy more, not seeing him at all, thinking and wondering where and how he was doing and most of all wondering where my siblings were.

Jack began to do things that were not good; he started having his friends come over and they would all go into the kitchen. I did not know what was taking place in there, but when Jack would come out, he wasn't be the same. After being in there for a while, they would all leave together, including Jack. This is when things really began to happen. Jack began doing things that I know wasn't pleasing to his family.

Ephesians 6;4, And, ye fathers, provoke not your children to wrath: but bring them up in the nurture and admonition of the Lord.

Robert, Jack Jr., and Antonio, Betty's three boys, were right behind each other, two, three, and four. My nephews had a fear of Jack just as Betty did. He would whoop them about anything, even for making too much noise while playing. When Jack was gone away from home, everything was fine; the children could play and Betty could talk louder. Betty would make sure Jack's food was prepared and she would make sure all her children and I would have eaten. Robert, Jack Jr., and I would jump around, laugh, and play without feeling that fear that we would get in trouble for playing. We didn't have to worry about Jack saying anything, but as soon as we heard Jack put the key in the door, we would sit down as if we were watching TV fearful of what he would say or do.

Things began to change day by day. I began to see more of Jack as far as how he treated Betty and my nephews. For me, he did not let me live there because he cared for my well-being, he only wanted to have his way with me. I only was twelve years old wanting only to be a child. The first time Jack tried to have his way with me was one night I was laying in my bed asleep and I awoke up to feeling something touching me on my private part. I awakened to see Jack over me. I began pushing his hand off me saying "Stop leave me alone," being very afraid, shaking and kicking my leg so he would leave me alone. He left me alone because he did not want to wake up Betty. I did not yell because I was frightened thinking that he would hurt Betty, my nephews and me. This caused me to really want my Daddy so he would keep me safe and secure from Jack.

I did not know or understand what Jack was trying to do because I never saw or heard of such things, but I know he was trying to do something bad to me.

The next morning while getting dressed for school, I went into the bathroom and made sure the door was closed tight and locked to keep Jack from coming in on me. Jack made lots of attempts to invade my private parts, but I would fight him off every time. I would try to stay awake at night to keep him from coming into my personal space. However, I thank God for keeping me safe, although he would some time put his finger into my private part. I looked for Betty to keep me safe as if she was Mama, but she was not aware of what he was doing to me.

Mrs. Simmons was such a nice teacher. I believe she had an idea that something was wrong, but she never asked any questions. In the afternoon, I would lay my head on my desk and fall asleep with both arms folded up under my head. Mrs. Simmons would let me sleep. Staying awake during the mornings was easy because I would be thinking and wondering where my Daddy, Melvin, Bernice, Carl, and Danny could have gone, wanting to be with them wherever they were.

I still did not have the best of clothes, I would wear the same clothes over and over. Betty did always make sure I had clean clothes even though I had to wash them out with my hands and hang them on the back porch to dry or on hangers in the kitchen. Mrs. Simmons asked if she could take me home after school one day. I told her I had to ask my sister. She began to tell me why she wanted to take me home with her; she said that she had some clothes to give me that her daughter couldn't wear anymore. I was so happy to get some different cloths even if they weren't brand new. The excitement of getting some different clothes was overwhelming. I was willing to take a chance of something worse than what Jack was doing to me to get them.

But then again, Mrs. Simmons was such a trust worthy and pleasant woman at school, I felt that I can trust her. She stayed right around the corner from the school just as she said. When we pulled in front of her house my eyes were so amazed, I thought we had pulled up in front of a movie star's home. I was thinking to myself these are some beautiful homes on this street. She unlocked her front door, I walked in and stood by her living room door as she hurried into another room. Mrs. Simmons came back with a big trash bag of clothes. I was so happy; I couldn't wait to get home to see what kind of clothes were in the bag. We got back in the car and she dropped me off at the house. I told her thank you just as Daddy taught me.

Betty was sitting on her bed; we opened up the bag and began pulling out every piece of clothing as if I had gone shopping. Mrs. Simmons had given me some pretty clothes and one pair of pretty shoes. Everything she gave me fit; her daughter must have been around my size and age. I thank God and Mrs. Simmons for the clothes.

Ruth 2:12 AMP, May the Lord repay you for your kindness, and may your reward be full from the Lord, the God of Israel, under whose wings you have come to take refuge.

Jack would still have his friends coming in and out and Betty still sounded afraid and timid when Jack talked to her. I remember the day Daddy came to check on Betty and me. He came in the door and I moved fast to hug him, as if I had lost something and found it in Daddy. I was so glad to see him. I felt like I did when Daddy would come home on Dickson St. except now I was too old to grab hold of his leg. Jack was not there that day. Daddy stood and talked to Betty for a while. He didn't stay long and before I knew it, he was gone again. I felt very sad the day after Daddy had come by. I couldn't tell him about what was going on because I feared Daddy would have killed Jack. I kept my feelings inside and went to go play with Robert, Jack Jr., and Antonio. That was the last time Daddy came to Jack and Betty's apartment.

Psalm 3:3, But thou, O Lord, art a shield for me; my glory, and the lifter up of mine head.

I can recall one night while lying in my bed, Jack closed the two sliding doors that separated the middle room from the front room. I could hear Jack moving around that night. I covered my head up and closed my eyes and rolled up in a ball pulling my knees up toward my chest and began to pray to God saying, "Lord please don't let him bother me."

Psalm 46:1, God is our refuge and strength, a very present help in trouble.

God answered my prayers because he did not bother me that night. Shortly after that, Jack's sister bought Norma Jean to stay with us. I was so glad to have Norma Jean with me again as I felt safe hoping Jack would not attempt to try anything again. It was good having her there even if she did make up tales about what she did.

I don't know what happened to Norma Jean while she lived with Jack's sister, but she began to pick at me wanting to fight for no reason. I didn't mind just as long as I had my sister with me. Betty would stand between us and make us sit down and sometimes tell Norma Jean, "If you want to fight, fight me." Betty would ball up her fist at Norma Jean as if she was going to box her. We would all stop and laugh. Other than that, we got along well.

One evening while everyone sitting watching television as usual, Jack came into the room and said, "Debbie come and go next door with me and help me get these pipes out of the apartment." The apartment he was referring to was empty and next door to us. Both back porches were connected with a small railing. The back door was already unlocked and all Jack did was turn the knob to open it. I thought I was really going to help get space heater pipes; I had no idea of what was going to take place. I didn't really think anything of it at first, even though, he didn't ask Betty, Norma Jean, or four-year-old Robert.

We entered the dark apartment through the kitchen. He walked in front of me as we went into the room where the space heater was. There sat a space heater, but the pipes were still connected to the stove. That's when my mind began to think that he was not going to get any space heater pipes. Jack pulled me to the floor and laid on top of me. I fought hard by kicking and swinging my hands. Despite my efforts, he was able to get his hands down into my pants and with his fingers he violated me. His actions not only caused physical hurt, but also emotional drama. He eventually stopped and yelled at me saying, "Get out of here." I hurried out the door, climbed back over the railing, walked back in the room where everyone was sitting, and began watching television.

Oh, how embarrass and dirty I felt. Norma Jean said aloud, "Debbie how did you get all that dirt in your head?" The only thing I wanted to do was not be seen by Betty and get far away from Jack as I possibly could. I did not respond to her question only to feel hurt in my heart. I thank God for keeping me from the predator that Betty had for a boyfriend. Betty sat on her bed as if she didn't have a clue what just happen not asking anything about the dirt that Norma Jean saw in my heir. I went immediately into the room and hoped no one would see or hear me crying.

A Saturday, not too long after that incident, I got dressed to go play with my friend that lived on the corner. I started to walk toward her house, but instead I just sat on a hard stomp looking up at the bright sunshine thinking and saying to myself, "There's got to be a God. How is the sun staying in the sky and how is it staying so bright?" That's when I started to realize in my heart saying to myself once again, "There's got to be a God." I thought to myself, when Jack would bother me, is God hearing me call for His help? I finally realized that God did hear me because He would give me the strength to fight as hard as I could, pushing and squirming this grown man off me. He also didn't want Betty to know what he was trying to do to me. I later found out that Jack had a drug addiction and this too probably attributed to me being able to fight him off.

I found out that Jack was doing drugs by accident. He had just come in with his friends and as usual they all went into the kitchen. I went to the restroom. By me being clueless about why they went into the kitchen and the restroom being next to the kitchen, no one paid me any attention when I looked into the kitchen. I was completely blown away by what I saw. I saw Jack with a piece of rubber around his arm and a needle sticking in his arm. Jack's friends were all sitting around waiting until their turn. I never saw such things or heard of such things before that night. After I came out of the restroom I went back into the front room as if I saw nothing.

Jack kept trying to molest me. I will never forget the day when Betty had to go to the grocery store. From time to time she would let Robert, Norma Jean and I walk with her, but this particular morning Betty woke up got herself dressed. I could hear Jack and her moving around and talking while she was getting dressed. I could hear Jack asking Betty if she was going to the store. I could hear Betty say yes. Jack began to ask who she was going to take with her. Betty replied that she was going to take Norma Jean and me. When I heard the word "store" and my name, I jumped out of bed thinking to myself, let me hurry and get my clothes on so that I can go to the store. I rushed to the restroom before Norma Jean could get up. Once I was dressed, Norma Jean got herself dressed and Betty bought Robert clothes in the room so that he could get dressed.

Suddenly I heard Jack say to Betty, "Keep Debbie here so that she can watch Jack Jr. and Antonio." Betty as usual said, "Ok, come on Norma Jean and Robert." I felt so bad that I could not go with Betty to the store knowing that when she left out the door I would be left there alone with Jack. When Betty left out the door with Norma Jean, and Robert I went back into the room where Jack Jr. and Antonio were sleeping. I began looking out the window watching Betty, Norma Jean, and Robert walk down the street heading toward the grocery store. I continued looking out the window watching every car that passed by hoping Betty would not take too long. Next thing I knew, Jack called me saying "Debbie come her?" I thought to myself, I'm facing this monster once again uncertain of what he was going to do. I was shaking as if he was going to kill me, but this time as I walked slowly toward the room he called out once more. Being obedient I walked toward him. He reached out, grabbed my arm, and pulled me closer to his side of the bed. I pushed him back from me and back to the room with Jack Jr. and Antonio where sleeping and began looking out the window once more really hoping and praying for Betty's return home. When Betty, Norma Jean, and Robert returned home, they had bags of food and by this time Jack Jr. and Antonio were woke. Jack was up and dressed as if nothing happened.

Later that morning, Jack's sister came over to see if she could take Norma Jean to watch her daughter. Betty, like usual, agreed. As soon as Jack's sister left with Norma Jean, Jack began to act out how he felt toward me for not letting him take advantage of me. I will never forget standing in the kitchen with Betty while she prepared to cook Jack's food. Jack came from the bedroom into the kitchen where Betty and I were. I was sitting in a chair asking Betty if I could stay home from school on Monday to go with a girl down the street to a dance show. Jack came in the kitchen saying, "Betty give me a glass of water." Jack heard me and Betty talking about the tv dance show but interrupted and asked Betty again for the water. He asked a third time, "Betty give me a glass of water!" in a firm, deep mean voice. I thought Jack wanted to drink the water, but instead as I was getting up from my seat to walk out the kitchen Jack took the glass of water and threw it right in my face. Jack began to tell Betty, "She has to go. Send her with the rest of them!"

Water was dripping from my face. Jack took me by surprise and I was shocked to know that he would do such a thing in front of Betty. I hurried toward the bedroom where Robert, Jack Jr. and Antonio were playing quietly. I tried not to let them see me crying nor my hurt.

When that Monday came I begged Betty once more about the dance until she approved of me skipping school and going. I hurried down the steps, ran to the corner where Denise lived, and I knocked on the door. I blotted out, "I can go!" She gave me her pants and I hurried to get dressed, before Jack could find out where I was going. Not wanting Betty to change her mind, after getting dressed I hurried down to Denise's house and her mother dropped us off at the tv station. The dance did not air until that following Saturday.

The Saturday that the dance show was scheduled to air, Norma Jean asked Betty if we could spend the weekend at Aunt Doris and Uncle Tommy's house. Betty approved and Norma Jean and I began to gather what we were going to wear for the weekend. This was the first time we would be spending the weekend at Aunt Doris and Uncle Tommy's house since we were little. This was also my first time seeing Carl and Danny again sense Jack and Betty moved from Fairground Place. Going to Uncle Tommy's house seemed fun at first. Saturday morning came and after everyone had gotten up and dressed, Aunt Doris made sure we all ate breakfast. Immediately after breakfast, everyone hurried to watch television so they could see me on the dance show.

Once the dance show came on everyone was sitting around in Aunt Dori's living room looking at the television. Everyone tried to spot me doing my dance moves. It was hard because the dance floor was crowded full of young people dancing. I was seen only twice out of the whole show. Aunt Doris said, "I saw her both times." I sat there feeling as if I was a movie star, knowing everyone was excited to see me on television even though it was only a few times. That was one time I felt very important because my family saw me on tv.

Returning home that Sunday was scary. Betty asked me if I had seen Willie and asked him if I could stay with him. I did not answer, thinking to myself what I am going to do now. Betty took me to Denise's house to call Uncle Tommy and ask him to come and get me and take me over to Willie's house. I was torn, on one hand I was happy I was getting away from the mental and sexual abuse that Jack put me through, but on the other hand I did not want to leave Robert,

Jack Jr., and Antonio knowing that he was abusing them. All I could do was ask God to keep them safe.

I thank God for hearing my prayers and putting it in Jack's heart to tell Betty to send me over to Willie's house.

1 John 5:15, And if we know that he hear us, whatsoever we ask, we know that we have the petitions that we desired of him.

When I came from Denise's house where I called Uncle Tommy, I went straight to the front room window and began looking out, waiting impatiently with excitement knowing that I could now see Carl and Danny anytime. At the same time, my heart was saddened because I knew I would not see Betty, Robert, Jack Jr., or Antonio for a while. Once Uncle Tommy came, I jumped up from the window, hugged Robert, Jack Jr., and Antonio, said bye to Betty and hurried down the steps with my trash bag.

I only stayed at Willie's house for a week, but it seemed a lot longer. Willie and his girlfriend did not care what Bernice, Carl, or Danny did or where they went. They had a lot of freedom since Daddy was not checking on them as much as before. I did not feel very comfortable there; Willie and his girlfriend did not get along and they would fight and yell at each other all the time. Willie's girlfriend did not keep the apartment clean and tidy. She would also whoop their little son, Willie Jr., very hard. I didn't like seeing that happen as it brought back memories of Jack whooping Robert, Jack Jr., and Antonio. After that week, Bernice had her boyfriend come and got Carl, Danny, and me. We were all together again and would be staying with Chucky and his girlfriend. Everyone, but Melvin and Betty. Melvin had enlisted in the Armed Forces. We were reunited, but there were still many troubles ahead.

Chapter 7

Reunited but Still Many Troubles on Eads Street

I was glad to be back living with my sisters and brothers on a regular basis. Bernice, Norma Jean, Carl, Danny, and I lived with Chucky and his girlfriend, Evelyn, who were living with their two children, her mother, two brothers, sister, and nephew. So once more we lived in a small crowded house.

Medea, Evelyn's mother, was a nice lady and she welcomed us when we arrived. However, she was the type of person that wanted things done her way or there would be repercussions. It didn't take much for her to become upset and start cursing and yelling. I recall shortly after moving in Larry, Evelyn's nephew, came out of the house and showed Norma Jean, Carl, Danny, and I the newspaper and Medea was on the front page. She had been arrested for pulling a gun on a man for not taking her to the store to cash her government check. This brought back memories of seeing Willie's face in the paper.

Evelyn had a brother that was wheelchair bound and didn't say much. His room was on the first floor of the house and it looked just like hospital room. It had a hospital bed and equipment set up in there for when his nurse would visit. I later found out that he had to have both of his legs amputated. The unsettling thing was they did it a little bit at a time. In between surgeries he had to keep his legs wrapped in bandages. Larry was also handicapped; his legs were not straight. But that didn't keep him from running and playing with us and the kids in the neighborhood.

We didn't live with Medea very long. No too long after moving in with them we moved out into a duplex on Park Ave. The upstairs unit was vacant which allowed Willie and his girlfriend to move upstairs with their two boys. Now we were really reunited apart from Betty and Melvin. We would go upstairs to visit often. Things had not changed much; Willie and his girlfriend still argued and fought a lot, she also still didn't keep the house clean. Willie started drinking a lot with his friends.

But he wasn't the only one. Chucky and Evelyn drank a lot and would go out every weekend. While residing on Park Ave. Evelyn had two more children, totaling four. She started going out by herself which caused arguments between her and Chucky. I hated to see them quarrel. Chucky would get so upset, he would cry from his frustration.

To keep from seeing the arguments and being the babysitter for Evelyn's four children, Norma Jean would call Uncle Tommy, my mother's brother-in-law, to come and get us for the weekend. We had not stayed with Aunt Doris and Uncle Tommy before, so I was not aware of who he was, a child predator just like Jack. Uncle Tommy would attempt to force himself on me just like Jack did. On one occasion, he called me downstairs while all the other children were playing upstairs. When I went to see what he wanted he began to fondle my breast. I pushed his hand away and ran back upstairs with everyone else. No one even noticed that I was gone. I remember wanting to cut my breast off because they were drawing attention to me that I didn't like or want.

On a different weekend stay, Aunt Doris and Uncle Tommy had some guests over. All the children were outside playing while the adults were in the house drinking and talking. I went into the house to use the restroom. As I was coming out of the restroom, Uncle Tommy was coming out of his bedroom, when he seen me he grabbed me and pushed me into his room onto the floor. He tried to force himself on me, but I kicked and pushed just like I did when Jack had me in the vacant house. He eventually let me go and thank God, he never tried to molest me again.

I was too afraid to tell Daddy or anyone what he had done to me because I knew what would have happened.

Spending the weekends at Aunt Doris and Uncle Tommy's house became pleasant again until their nephew, who was just released from jail, violated me. After everyone had gone to bed, their nephew came into the room where all the girls slept. I was the first person that he came to in the dark. As he grabbed me he told me to get up right now. He gripped me so tight that the pain caused me to yell out. My yelling awakened everyone in the room and Uncle Tommy. I remember very vividly Uncle Tommy telling him, "Come out of this room and leave them girls alone!" He ran back across the hall to the room he was sleeping in. The next morning Uncle Tommy told him he had to leave. After that incident I never wanted to go over to their house again, and we never did, but I was also so tired of grown men trying to take advantage of me.

A little while later Bernice became pregnant and moved in with her boyfriend across the street from us in apartment over an old business. She didn't have much, but we liked visiting with her. After she had her baby boy, Peter, we would take turns spending the night to help her out. My older siblings continued to drink and party on the weekends. There was still a lot of arguing and fighting among Willie and his girlfriend as well as Chuck and Evelyn. Once Chucky and Willie actually told Norma Jean and I to fight a couple of girls that had called us b@#$*&^. Fighting was no longer an uncommon thing.

Before I was able to finish the eighth grade, we moved again; to a two-family flat on Eads St. about two blocks from Medea. Larry would come over Chucky and Evelyn's house every day with one of Evelyn's brothers, Wallace. Wallace was the type of boy that stayed in trouble with the law. Larry was not as bad as Wallace; he just liked aggravating everyone.

One night while playing outside, Wallace was coming across the lot next to the two-family flat, Norma Jean, two girls from the neighborhood, and I were playing on the sidewalk in front of the girls' house. Wallace was a dangerous boy and he enjoyed playing with guns. It seemed as if once we made eye contact with him as he was coming across the lot, he shot the gun toward us. I know God was with us that night because the bullet from the gun came right between Norma Jean and me. We actually saw fire as we heard the loud pop. We all ran onto the porch in fear. As Wallace walked up, we asked him why he did that. He laughed and said that he didn't do anything. The girls' mother came outside because she heard the shot. Wallace kept on walking down the street as if nothing had happened. By the grace of God no one was hurt that night.

The family; Chucky, Evelyn, their four children, Norma Jean, Carl, Danny, and I moved once more right after my eighth-grade graduation. Chucky's run-in with the police forced us to leave the Southside of St. Louis, MO and move to the Northside of town. On the Northside is when my life really took a change of direction.

Chapter 8
Life Begins with Jim on Emerson Street

The area we relocated to on the Northside was a mixed neighborhood with black and white people, which was new to us. Once we were all moved in and situated, Norma Jean, Carl, Danny, and I would sit out on the long porch looking to see if there were any other children living in the neighborhood. Evelyn quickly got to know one of the neighbors across the street from us. Before we knew it, we all knew the entire family and they were a very nice family. Mrs. Lucy and Mr. Big Lee, what everyone called him, had three boys and four girls. Their children ranged in ages that were close to ours.

Mrs. Lucy was a stay at home mom and Mr. Big Lee worked full-time. The first time going to their house was like a whole new world to me. It looked as if they were wealthy and wanted for nothing; they had a beautiful home. The oldest girl invited us to her room to sit and listen to the record player. I did find it strange that the children called their mother by her name, Lucy, and their father, Big Lee, instead of saying mama and daddy. I was not used to hearing children call their parents by their name. To me, it seemed like the perfect house and they were the perfect family. I enjoyed spending time there.

When I met my soon-to-be husband, I had no intentions on dating him. I had dated a boy from the old neighborhood who went away to the armed forces; I was only fifteen when we began dating. He would write letters to me saying that he loved me, but I could not understand how you could love someone and leave them. I really didn't understand much about love and I still thought that I was the ugliest girl around. I had the notion that all the boys wanted from me was to get close to me just to do what Jack and Uncle Tommy had done to me. I genuinely only wanted a boyfriend to have a boy around for a few hours to hang out with, without us having sex, and then he could go home. I wanted to be loved by someone. One of the letters I received from the boy that went into the armed forces asked if I would marry him. I didn't write him back because once again I did not want to live a grown-up life. In fact, I never wrote him again.

During my freshman year, I met a boy and we began dating. The relationship lasted for quite some time and I sincerely had feelings for him. But he too wanted to do things I was just not ready to do. So, I ended the relationship. Things at home were not on the best of terms. Evelyn was expecting her fifth child and Norma Jean and I had to take turns on missing school to watch their children. Even though Evelyn was receiving public assistance for us, she did not spend the cash on our needs. Yes, she would ensure that we had food to eat, but we didn't have the clothes. I was seventeen years old and a sophomore in high school. Not having the clothes that I wanted, my self-esteem was low.

During this time a new family moved to the same block as us, just a couple of houses down the street. This family was a lady that had six children and she had two of her brothers staying with her one was my age going to the same school and the other was eight years older than me staying with his sisters working a job. Chucky knew this family from way back when we all went to Greater Paradise Church.

I would walk pass this house on my way home from school. Jim, the brother that was eight years older, would sit and watch me pass by everyday saying things to make me blush and smile, nothing provocative. He would let me know that I was a beautiful young lady. Things were still bad at home so after completing my homework and chores in the house, instead of going across the streets to talk to Lucy's daughters, I would go and sit on the porch with Jim at his sister's house. Before I knew it, our conversations would be lengthy, and we talked about everything under the sun. I told him about my life and he shared his story with me. I was not trying to have a relationship with him. I had just broken up with my boyfriend and I needed someone to talk to, but by me sitting and talking to him every evening Evelyn began telling Chucky that she thought I was going with Jim. However, she was wrong, that was the farthest thing from my mind. I was longing for the boyfriend that I had.

One day after school upon walking into the living room, Chucky and Evelyn were sitting there waiting to talk to me about sitting on the porch and talking to Jim. They assumed that I was having a relationship with him. I understood why they were concerned because he was eight years older than me; I was only seventeen and he was twenty-five and that was a great difference in age. They questioned me about Don, my ex-boyfriend. They wanted to know why we broke up and I was not in the mood to discuss the details. This whole ordeal really upset me.

After school the next day Jim was sitting on the porch as I walked by as usual. He asked me to come here for a minute, but I told him I would be out later. I was still feeling like I had lost my best friend after the conversation with Chucky and Evelyn. That evening I sat on our porch not wanting to talk to anyone. Jim did not come outside while I was sitting on the porch, so I built up enough nerve to go across the street and knock on his door to see what was he doing. I needed someone to talk to and he was the only one I could talk to. Once he came out I began telling him about what Evelyn and Chucky were saying. His reply was, "Sense they are saying that we are going together, let's make it true." I really didn't pay too much attention to his comment because I thought by Jim being older, all that was on his mind was the things that I was not ready for. I was determined that I was not going to let anyone else take advantage of me or give myself to anyone until I was married.

The conversation with Chucky and Evelyn cause me to increasingly think about my ex-boyfriend. It made me contemplate getting back with him. The next day I tried to find him at school. I wanted him to see me, but when I found him, he wouldn't speak to me or pay me any attention. This made me feel even lonelier and caused me to believe that no one wanted me.

As time passed I found myself hanging out with Jim more. He seen that I was wearing the same clothes over and over. Things changed for us when he asked me could he take me shopping for some new clothes and shoes. Initially, I didn't want to go with him, but I knew not to depend on Evelyn to take me shopping. Due to the earlier false accusations, I had a "I don't care" attitude". So, I began seeing Jim every day and allowed him to buy me things. Before I knew it, I started telling people we were a couple. This caused Evelyn to become extremely upset with me; I don't think that she truly cared about my well-being or what happened to me. I believe that she was more concerned about possibly losing the government assistance she was getting for me.

Evelyn eventually dropped out of nursing school and began not staying at home. She and Chucky were arguing more and more and things began to fall apart with their relationship. Evelyn started staying out all night. As time went on, we would come home from school and there would be strange men sitting in our house, friends of Evelyn. But the day came when I decided to leave home, I will never forget that moment.

I came in the house from school that evening feeling depressed because everything seemed to be taking a hold of me. All I wanted to do was be with Jim, the only man that showed me love at a time that I needed it the most. I came in the house with a made-up mind that I was leaving. I told this to Evelyn and she said, "No you are not going anywhere!" Chucky inquired asking me, "Why do you want to leave? What are we doing to you? What is it that you want?" I couldn't put into words all that I felt and all that was causing me to be overwhelmed. Me not answering Chucky brought him to tears. Again, he asked, "What is it that you want?" All I could bellow out was, "I am tired of not having anything and not being able to go anywhere." I ran to my room crying and started packing my clothes.

Evelyn told Chucky to leave me alone and let me leave. So, I walked out of the house and across the street with a few of my clothes. I knocked on the door and Jim answered it. I explained to him what had just taken place and he asked his sister could I stay there with them until he was able to get us an apartment of our own. Daddy was not upset with the decision that I had made; he sent Bernice to let me know that I was grown in his eyes. I was with Jim for thirty-five years.

Chapter 9
Life Continues on Alcott Street

After being at Jim's sister house for several days, Jim realized that I was not going to go back to Evelyn's and Chucky's house. This brought about a change in Jim that I didn't expect. His true personality came out of hiding. Over those several days, I met Jim's family as they visited his sister's house often.

In my heart I knew I was not ready to face grown up decisions, because I stilled desired to play with my younger brothers and Mrs. Lucy's daughters. And in my teenage thinking, I began to talk with Jim's niece about personal things when she would come down into the basement. She revealed to me how her mother's male friend was not treating her appropriately. Being in similar situations, I felt that I could give her some sound advice. I didn't think that she would ever go back and tell her mother what I had said to her. But she did, and this was the beginning of 35 years of abuse by Jim.

Jim's sister told him what I had said to his niece. Apparently, this made him quite upset. He called me upstairs from the basement and before I knew it, he had struck me in the face. He never asked me what was actually said; he just reacted in this manner. I would never had thought that Jim would do this to me, especially in front of his family. But he did. His mother came from the kitchen and began yelling, "You stop hitting her before you wind up back in jail!"

I went back into the basement, laid on the bed, and began crying and feeling betrayed by Jim. I felt like my whole world had fallen from beneath me. At that moment, I needed a hug from my daddy and to hear that everything would be alright. I just wanted to let him know that I wasn't as grown as I thought I was. I was too embarrassed to go back across the street to my family, so I stayed. Jim eventually came down into the basement and told me how sorry he was and promised that he would never do that again. He began kissing me and this made me feel loved once again.

I continued to attend school during our time at Jim's sister house. As I walked through the halls, it was my desire to run into Don and magically our relationship would be rekindled. This would give me the opportunity to end things with Jim and return home to my family. Unfortunately, that didn't happen and as time passed Jim started revealing more of his true character. He would go out drinking with his sister's friend and leave me alone in the basement. He lost his job at the hotel and found another one at a furniture store. The people he met through his new job liked to gamble. Jim joined them when they would go out on the weekends. He began to drink more and became addicted to gambling.

Eventually, Jim found us a place to live which was right around the corner from Emerson Street, just walking distance from his sister and Chucky's house. Oh, how excided I was to have my own apartment. This was unbelievable for me; I had mixed emotions. I felt like I was grown having grown-up responsibilities, but at the same time I wanted to be a teenager playing in the streets. I felt I needed a job instead of school because I thought about how we were going to pay bills with Jim's gambling habit and his little pay check. After moving into our apartment, I started to feel as though Jim was my husband instead of my boyfriend.

Jim started asking me to cook breakfast for him. I had already known how to clean, as that's what Evelyn had us doing all the time, but the little cooking I did learn came from Jim's mother, who taught me while living with them. Things seemed to get easer and harder at the same time. I was still getting up for school early but wasn't really interested in any of my school assignments. I felt as if I was only going to school just to walk the halls and see if I could see Don. I genuinely wanted to turn back the hands of time. The only thing that stopped me was my pride; I worried what other's may say.

After school, while Jim was still at work, I would go around the corner to see Carl and Danny whom I missed very much. Sometimes they would come visit me at my place. One Friday after visiting my brothers, I came home to a drunk Jim. Jim's drinking problem had gotten much worse. His drinking would cause him to want to argue and fight me. On this occasion, Jim was upset because I was not home when he got there, and dinner was not ready. I opened the door to him yelling and questioning me. He demanded to know where I was and who I was with. He wanted to know why dinner was not ready. To keep peace, I didn't say anything, but I was thinking to myself: you can cook for yourself, I can go where ever I want to go, you are not my husband or my daddy. Jim became more controlling and violent as time went on.

One Saturday evening after loosing all of his money gambling, Jim came home drunk and upset. He begun to take his anger and frustrations out on me. He started yelling and cursing at me for no apparent reason. He began to strike me in the face causing my eye to swell and bruise. Our landlord lived right below and hearing the commotion called the police. Jim knew that if the officers seen my face in its current state that he would be arrested and back to jail he would go. Jim blocked the door preventing me from leaving the apartment. He thought that if we didn't come out of the apartment that eventually the police would leave. But they remained in their patrol car for quite some time. Jim finally open the door for us to leave together. As we walked down the stair, he begged me not to tell the police what had taken place. He repeatedly promised that it wouldn't happen again. While walking to his sister's house, Jim held my arm firmly to keep me close to him. I felt as though I had nowhere to go.

Once again, I fell for Jim's smooth talk. I never reported to the police what had happened that night and things only got worse from that point. Jim and I began moving from house to house because we didn't have enough money to keep the bills paid. I ended up dropping out of school and getting a job. I was only making minimum wages and Jim would take that with his money and spend it on liquor, gambling, and partying. At some point, Jim stopped working and started collecting copper pipes from old houses to junk. This didn't help to make ends meet. So, we wound up moving back in with his family.

Not much time had passed before I became pregnant with out first child. I really hoped that being pregnant would make Jim love me and the abuse would stop. I thought that having a child would cause him to stop drinking, partying, and gambling. Jim was so happy to be bringing his first child into the world, but nothing changed. I was able to get into a program that would help me get my GED and assist me in finding a job. After finding my job, it was hard to keep studying for my GED, so I dropped out of the program. On the brighter side, I was able to keep that job for over five years. On the other hand, Jim kept going from job to job. Over the next eight years we had three more children and even though they brought great joy and happiness to us, Jim was still emotionally, verbally, and physically abusive to me.

Chapter 10
Life with Jim on Many Streets

It wasn't hard for me to make friends on my new job. In fact, meeting new people on the job made me feel as though I had a whole new family. It was nice being around people other than Jim's family. We were so close that one of the ladies I worked with planned a baby shower for me. Unfortunately, it was canceled because I was placed on bed rest in the later part of my pregnancy. The doctor diagnosed me with Toxemia or better known as pre-eclampsia. While carrying our baby, Jim didn't hit me. He would only raise his voice during arguments. That didn't bother me as much as long as there was no physical abuse. It has been said that stress can cause Toxemia. Despite the fear of something going wrong, God had everything in the palm of His hands. My first child was born healthy without any complications.

After giving birth, my job moved its location from in the city of St. Louis to one of the suburbs. The relocation made for a difficult commute as I had no one to drive me back and forth to work and at this point I had not learned to drive. I was unable to return to this job after my maternity leave was over.

After losing my job, times became hard on Edgewood Street. Jim promised that things were going to be different and he acted as if he was going to be a great father. He decided to try and buy a house; we even got the money for the down payment. He knew that this was a dream of mine seeing as though I moved so much as a child and early in our marriage. I was so excited about buying this house. It was located in an area that I believed would be a great neighborhood to raise our child. I felt that being around civilized people would enhance our lives. Needless to say, we never bought the house.

Jim couldn't keep a stable job, so he decided to become a cab driver. This was his way of making ends meet. This also was his way of having reliable transportation. Jim still had a gambling and drinking problem and couldn't keep the bills paid. The winter after Little Jim's first birthday, we were without electricity for over a week. It wasn't until I received my income tax check that we were able to get caught up on the bills. It was also during these times of extra funds that Jim was more pleasant.

My heart cried out to God to free me from the agony of waking up each day not knowing if our bills were going to be paid, not knowing if we were going to have to move again. I felt like the little girl back in time on Dickson Street not having necessities. I never wanted my children to suffer the same way I had to as a child. God heard my cries and while things didn't change in that manner right away, He let me know that He was still right there with me. One evening Jim was heading out to go gambling and drinking. He asked me if I wanted to go with him; he never invited me before. Initially I told him no. Then he asked again, and I agreed to go with him that night. After I accepted his invitation, he suggested that I go visit one of my sisters. I told him that I wanted to go with him instead of making a trip to their houses. When we returned home, we found that someone had broken into our house trashing it and stealing a few of our items. Whoever broke in left a knife on the night stand beside the bed. God had sent His angles once again to watch over me. I thank Him I was not there even though I was with Jim at the gambling house.

Jim and I continued to move from place to place. We moved from a fixer upper to an apartment. From an apartment to a house. From a house to an apartment. Finding out that I was having another child with Jim was so hard for me. I felt stuck with him; like I would never be free. Discovering we were having our fourth child did something to Jim. It was at this time in our marriage that we resided at the same place for the longest time, five years. He also kept his job driving cabs and I became a stay at home mom. While the children where in school I tried going back to school getting a trade in secretarial, but that didn't pan out. I also tried working odd jobs, and they too didn't last long.

Over the years Jim and I would still visit Norma Jean and her husband along with Carl, Danny, Evelyn and Chucky. Briefly during the five-year residence at our home, my sister Norma Jean and her children came to stay with us. She and her husband separated, and it left her needing a place to stay. I was happy to be able to help my sister out.

Shortly after Norma Jean and her children found a place and moved out, I began to feel weak. We had moved again ourselves to Union Street. I felt so discombobulated. I would join Jim when he was drinking. I would drink to forget about my problems. This was not in my character, but it did allow me to keep things off my mind. This didn't last long; I had to get a grip on what I was doing to me and my babies. I realized one of us had to be there for our children.

Norma Jean moved close by and I was able to visit her and her children. I wanted so badly to leave Jim; not because of the physical abuse. I wanted to leave him because he couldn't keep a decent roof over our heads. We had to move yet again. The next house we lived in was a big three-story house. It was after this move that I cried out to the Lord to please help me. I didn't know when nor how the relief was going to come, but I had faith that He would someday bring it.

Moving homes wasn't the only moving we did. Jim changed churches and we began going to a church called Light of Jericho. This church was a small church, but it had a great pastor and great members. Jim began to get acquainted with the members of the church. He also became close to the pastor. Not long after we become members, Jim became Assistant Pastor. Unfortunately, this didn't stop us from going out on the weekends partying. It also didn't stop him from gambling, drinking, or the abuse.

Living in the three-story house became a burden to Jim and me. He was tired of me complaining about our bills not being paid because of his gambling and drinking. Despite me working a temporary job at a warehouse, it still wasn't enough. We move again to a small apartment. With getting our income tax return, we were able to move and buy me a car. Jim sent me to driving school so I would be able to drive myself to work.

Chapter 11
Life Changes on the Poplar St. Bridge

Moving from one place to another, things began to get worse in our marriage. I was working then coming home everyday living in a four-room apartment not knowing which way to go. There was not enough room in the apartment to still away and study my Bible. Nonetheless, I was determined to etch out space for me. I used a small space at the kitchen window and sat a chair in front of it. The area provided great light. I would make it my business to come home from work before everyone else and read my Bible. I was very diligent in praying and asking God to help me understand what I was reading. This became my daily routine; read, pray, and listen to gospel music.

I had been seeking God to fix me and I didn't know how He was going to do it. This was a time in my life when everything seemed to be falling apart. A couple of days before the Fourth of July, Jim asked me to ride with him to get some fireworks for our son and grandchildren. Reluctantly I said yes; I really wanted to stay home to continue reading my Bible. Once we left the apartment and started on the highway all I could think of was what I was reading about in the Bible. Jim was talking to me about a little bit of everything, but I was not paying him much attention. My mind kept thinking about the word of God.

The location we were heading to purchase the fireworks was in E. St. Louis, IL. The city was just across the bridge and when we arrived there were numerous tents set up selling fireworks. We walked from tent to tent picking out fireworks that we thought Arthur, our son, would like to light. After Jim purchased our items, we headed back home using the same highway. Soon after getting on the highway, a car coming from the opposite direction crossed over the yellow line and hit us. Jim had been drinking on this evening and I, still to this day, believe the driver of that car was too. Our car went spinning around and hit the retaining wall. The driver of the other car didn't stop. He just kept going. The driver of a different car that witnessed the accident, stopped to see how he could help.

Jim assured the good Samaritan that he was all right. I on the other hand was trapped in the car. I could hear the sirens of the ambulance as it arrived on the scene. Jim kept asking me if I was all right. I continually reassured him that I was fine. As soon as the paramedics arrived they immediately rescued me from the car. At that time, the only thing I thought was wrong was the scrape on my leg from being wedged under the dashboard. Jim was not injured and was able talk to the police about what had happened as well as give them a description of the car that hit us.

The EMT's loaded me into the ambulance and we proceeded to the nearest hospital which was on the Illinois side of the river. I could hear Jim and one of the paramedics talking and the sound of the ambulance racing over the road. In the ambulance, I didn't feel any pain other than my leg. I assumed that a quick exam would be all that was needed, and Jim and I would be on our way back home. However, after arriving to the Emergency Room and the nurses doing their assessments, one nurse pulled Jim to the other side of the room. I couldn't understand and answer some of her questions. I could hear her asking Jim, "Does she normally talk like that?" Jim's reply was, "No!" Their voices were fading in and out.

I felt the stretcher moving down the hallway and next I knew I was being loaded into an ambulance. I could hear the sirens, but everything started fading in and out. I don't remember arriving at Barnes-Jewish Hospital. In fact, the only thing I do remember is vaguely being in the Intensive Care Unit with lots of machines, IV's in both arms, and the oxygen canula forcing oxygen up my nose. I wasn't aware of how much time had passed being unconscious in the ICU; I do remember hearing the doctor tell Jim that everyone should go home because I was not going to make it through the night. Thanks, be unto God, I made it through the night and sometime later was moved from ICU to a regular hospital room.

I continued to drift in and out of consciousness. I recall hearing Jim voice speaking to me saying, "Hey pretty girl!" I opened my eyes and I saw the face of him and my beautiful children standing around me. I could feel the love flowing from their hearts to mine. During times of awareness, I would try speaking to my loved ones, but they were unable to understand my speech. I loosely recall nurses coming in talking with me. They attempted to get me to eat, unfortunately I didn't know what "eat" meant. Doctors would come in and ask me if I could feel them sticking me with needles or hard objects; they would touch my feet with feathers. Regrettably, I was unable to feel anything on the left side of my body, I was paralyzed. I had suffered a head injury. I would also ask God to heal my body and help my family cope with what I was going through.

While I was hospitalized, tension rose between my siblings and Jim. Everyone wanted to know what happened that caused my brain injury because of the abuse in our marriage. Jim told them on many occasions that it was due to the car accident. They didn't believe him though. They would constantly insist on speaking with my treating doctors to see what caused the head injury. They were intrusive with the nursing staff and eventually they were restricted from visiting me in the hospital. It was quite challenging to only be able to see Jim, my children, and Pastor Rogers.

Pastor Rogers was my pastor from Light of Jericoh. I remember the day when Jim and our children were sitting around me. I began to ask them in a most demanding voice to call my pastor! Jim called Pastor Rogers asking him to come. He agreed, and I thank God for him leaving his family to come and be with me and my family. I remember hearing Pastor Rogers talking to Jim and the children. I was laying there not fully cognitive of what was going on and feeling dreadfully weak, but I did understand whenever Pastor Rogers talked about the Lord. I would nod my head "yes" and would say, "That's right." I believe God was allowing me to hear and understand the His word while still being very sick. Despite not always knowing what was going on around me or being able to communicate clearly with my family, I was persistent in praying in my heart and talking to God.

One evening while lying in my hospital bed I remember waking up yelling loudly at the top of my voice, "Thank You Jesus, Thank You Jesus, Thank You Jesus!" While lying there it seemed as though I was having an out of body experience. I recall climbing up on these big stars. I climbed from one star to the next star. As soon as I climbed on the last star I saw a large face. It was the face of a man and he was so handsome. I think it was one of God's angels; the strange thing about the beautiful face was he had on eye glasses. He had beautiful curly hair and a stunning smile. He smiled and winked his eye at me.

Before I knew it, I was coming up off a hard surface with my hand placed behind me as if I was lifting myself up from a hard floor. I had no feeling. I was numb. I didn't have any thoughts. My body just felt as if it was a shell with nothing in it. The next thing I saw was this big radiant light that was so bright I couldn't look directly at it. I dropped my head to shield my eyes from the intensity of the light. I endeavored to look once more, and I saw fog in front of the bright light. Immediately I heard the deepest voice imaginable. The voice was so deep and pleasant human language can't express the feelings of awe and wonder I beheld. In my heart I genuinely believe that this was the voice of God speaking to me.

God instructed me to write down what He was saying to me. I was disobedient when I woke up and didn't do what He told me to do. I thought that the memory of this encounter would be with me forever. So, needless to say, I didn't write it down and I don't remember what God told me. After yelling, "Thank You Jesus," three times Jim ran to get the nurse. I could hear the nurse and Jim talking. The nurse told him that sometimes when people have head injuries they either get extremely mean or religious. I thank God for my head injury, if that's what happened to me to help me to draw nearer to God. Afterwards things began to become a little clearer to me. I realized that I was in the hospital and on this earth.

That wonderful experience was the turning point in my recovery. I began noticing that when Jim would come visit me, I was able to hold a conversation with him. Initially I needed the assistance of a nurse to get to the restroom, but in no time, I was able to go on my own just using my IV pole for support. Since I couldn't comprehend the concept of eating, I received my nutrients through my IV, but after the experience with God's light I was blessed to have my taste buds awakened and be able to start eating again. Each day I got stronger and stronger. At the onset of the head injury, I was unable to take care of my personal hygiene. A nurse would have to give me a sponge bath daily, until one day I told the nurse I wanted to try taking a bath. She agreed, and we took the many small steps required for me to take a shower in the bathroom. Oh my, it was so refreshing.

Jim seeing the improvements I was making almost daily asked the doctors when would I be able to be discharged to return home. They explained to him that I wouldn't be able to go home I would have to be transferred to a rehabilitation center first. I don't know exactly how long my stay was at the hospital, but I was eventually moved to The Rehabilitation Institute of St. Louis.

One day I decided to get out of my bed and get in the wheelchair the nurse was keeping in my room for transport. I rolled myself down the hall near the nurse's station to an area that had a rail running along the wall. I began to pull myself up out of the wheelchair by holding on to the railing with both hands and began to walk. I walked like a baby just learning to walk for the first time. My nurse asked me what I was doing and my reply to her was, "I am trying to teach myself how to walk again." In a very nice voice she told me not to hurt myself and went back to work. I only took a couple of steps in one direction and then slowly back to my wheelchair. The nurse kept saying for me to take my time. She eventually got up from her chair and walked beside me making sure I didn't fall. Once I was back in the wheelchair, she rolled me into my room making sure I was back in my bed safely.

This was only the first step, I kept trying to do things on my own such as holding on to items in the room to go to the restroom and taking my own baths. Jim was so happy to know that I was trying to do things on my own regardless of still feeling terrible and weak. I continued asking God to bring me out of the effects of my head injury as I was ready to make decisions on my own.

Once I arrived at the rehab center, I was determined to get better as quickly as possible. I told God that I didn't want to stay this way. I wanted to start walking and comprehending things again. He answered my prayer by giving me strength and the willpower to press pass how weak I felt and the pain. Jim would visit almost daily and nearly every visit he would ask to speak to the doctor to see when I would be coming home. This made me feel that Jim really loved me and if I would go home everything would be all right and there would be no more abuse.

    Jim was told by a nurse that the doctors would be in to talk to him during rounds on this particular day. So, he made it to the rehab center right before breakfast waiting to talk to my doctor to see if I would be allowed to leave and go home. My doctor came in to my room and Jim asked him about me going home. I knew I wasn't well enough and needed to stay in the center longer. My doctor came in and I raised myself up in the bed, fixed my pillow to make myself sit up higher believing that this would fool the doctor. My doctor told Jim, "Your wife need to stay in the rehabilitation center a little longer." Jim said, "She seems to be doing better to me. I think if she was at home it would make her do a lot better being around me and the children." The doctor told him that I was a good actor, and wanted him to think that I was doing well, but he was willing to release me if Jim promised him that if something went wrong he would bring me back and that he would ensure that I got to therapy every day. Jim swore to my doctor that he would follow his guidelines to the letter. I wasn't released that day; however, I did get to go home much sooner than originally planned.

I don't remember exactly what day I was discharged from the center, but I remember Jim bringing me and my stuff from the hospital to our little apartment. Jim held me by my hand making sure that I wouldn't fall. He was doing everything the doctor told him to do. Once he opened the door of our apartment, I felt better immediately. Being able to see my children and grandchildren all sitting around to welcome me home. That was one happy day as we sat having so much fun. I imagined if I could keep them laughing, no one would think about my injury, and I would feel better. I thank God, I was able to do something doctors said I would never be able to do; I learned to walk again and regained my ability to comprehend information.

Chapter 12
Help on Union Street

After getting out of the hospital, I thought things would be better. Even though, we had to move from the two-bedroom apartment to another old house while Jim and his friend restored it for us to reside in, it didn't bother me if Jim was happy. I restarted working on my GED again, this time at another location, and retuned to taking care of my youngest son. I believed that Jim's drinking habit was resolved. He began treating me like a wife should be treaded. He put a lot of time into fixing the house and went out and purchased new future. Jim and I continued to attend church.

Disappointedly, Jim's old behaviors resurfaced. While cleaning I found a bottle of whisky hid beneath the towels in the lining closet. I didn't want to talk to Jim about this as I was afraid of what might happen. I felt that he would revert to fighting me again. But I built up enough courage to discuss the issue. Oh, what did I do that for? Jim started yelling at me, just as he did in the past, telling me that it didn't belong to him. On another occasion I was cleaning under the bed and I found another whisky bottle, but this time he told me, "I am grown. I can do what I want, and no one can tell me what to do." Jim stop hiding his drinking and began drinking openly in front of me and the children.

The very last time Jim abused me physically was while living at this location. One evening after coming home from Bible class with our youngest son, I was feeling very happy because the church had given me a small devotional Bible book. The book was in a small bag. Jim did not go to church that night, instead he stayed home drinking waiting for me to return. Just as I turned the door knob to open the door, Jim grab my bag and throw it across the room. It was so sudden I could only react by calling on God to save me. Jim assaulted me all night. I believe to this day that the enemy was trying to use Jim to kill me but, in my heart, I knew God was right there with me.

I was finally able to get free from Jim early the next morning. While running away from Jim I felt myself become weak from lack of sleep, stress, and the pain. As I ran across the street, I passed out. All I remember seeing was a beautiful lady that seemed to appear from out of nowhere. She mouthed to me did I need the police and I nodded yes. This lady had on a military uniform. The uniform was navy blue with a light blue-collar shirt. She wore a black military tie around the collar of her shirt. Her shoes were shiny black patent leather with no creases. Everything seemed to be perfect on this lady. The strange thing about her uniform was she had no medals, ribbons, nor a name tag on her jacket.

Jim attempted to lift me up off the ground as the lady walked up to us. He noticed her, then asked, "Can you watch her while I get my shoes and shirt?" Jim ran back to the house and I laid on the ground looking up at this lady. She never touched me. She just simply said in a sweet voice, "It is over. It is over. You never have to worry no more. It is over." I have wondered for years if God sent an angle to save me. Before I knew it, police and a fire truck came pulling up. I was able to get to a safe place and call my daughter. God blessed me with a new beginning.

Chapter 13

Peace in A Shelter

I didn't want to stay with my daughter and her family. I never wanted to be a burden on any of my children. I have always told my children that my door was open to them coming back home if they needed to. But I never thought that I would be going to live with them at their place of residence. I didn't want Jim to go to jail; I just wanted him to stay far away from me. I was told by my old pastor that love doesn't hurt. I knew that when I hurt my family hurt. I didn't know what to do or what to think. I was wondering how my family and friends would feel if I remained in that predicament. I began to feel lost and confused.

I thank God for my children being supportive of my decision to get the help I needed. It was hard. I started thinking about the material things I might lose. I didn't like not being able to sleep in my own bed and I missed being at home, regardless of how Jim treated me. But I knew in my heart if I went back, I would never be free from Jim and the abuse. I had to think about how God allowed me another opportunity to have a new beginning. I felt the need to be free from my hurt and pain. All I wanted to do is be able to live for Jesus telling others about how the light brought me through.

After staying with my daughter for two weeks, I knew I needed to decide whether I was going to move out of St. Louis with my middle son or stay here and make a life for my youngest son. I cried out asking God with tears flowing down my face, "God where do I go from here?" I obeyed to the voice of God when He told me to look in the phone book and call a shelter. The thought of staying in a shelter was new and the unknown was quite scary to me. I recalled a program I seen on television with people sleeping on cots and eating soup and bologna sandwiches. This was not at all what I wanted to do.

I confirmed that going to a shelter was really what the Lord wanted me to do. I called a few places and God opened the door for me at the right shelter. The lady that answered the phone was so pleasant. She told me they would be glad to send a cab for me. Shortly after doing an assessment on the phone the cab pulled up in front of the house. The time had come for me to say good-bye to my grandchildren. Thankfully it was close to summer and school was getting ready to end. The mother of Aaron's friend agreed to allow him to stay with her and her family until I got my own place. Aaron's godmother helped out with him while I was in the shelter as well. These two women alleviated so much stress knowing that my son was in good hands.

I was greeted as the cab pulled up by a lady outside of the building. Before I was able to get settled there were mounds of paperwork that I had to fill out. Being a shelter for domestic violence, I was to promise that I would reveal my location to anyone. As I sat in the office, my heart began to race as I thought about what was behind the big wooden door and how will these people treat me.

After getting behind the wooden door, I was taken to a room on the second floor to put my things away. There were many different races, ages, and nationality of women walking back and forth, up and down the hall. I began to feel lonely and depressed thinking about everyone including Jim, from time to time. I was hoping that my stay here would be over very soon. I never had to be in such a place feeling isolated from the entire world. I was looking at this place as an institution in a bad way, not knowing that it would be a help to me in the end.

I shared the room with a young lady. As I was putting my things away, she began to sob loudly. I inquired to why she was here at the shelter. She revealed to me that she was from out of town and desperately wanted to return home. I began to explain the best of my ability about my situation and letting her know about God and how He saved my life. I also told her that God heard her cries and knew what was best for her. I had finished putting my things away and took a shower. Once I got into bed, I began to ask the young lady did she know how to pray. She responded with a no. I told her to close your eyes and

I would pray with her. After praying I told her everything would be all right and time would go by fast.

The way the program was arranged, participants were to remain in the house for about six months. This time would give us the opportunity to be introduced to all the government programs available to us to give us the help that we needed to start over. Different people from the various agencies would come into the center to discuss the benefits of their programs. Over the six months that I was there, I became very acquainted with the staff and other women living there. It began to feel less like a prison and more like a safe place. I learned some great values in this shelter.

I would remain in contact with my pastor. I had made up in my mind that I would never stop going to church or serving God. In keeping with the rules, I would meet my pastor's wife around the corner from the shelter. She would come and pick me up to attend church on Wednesdays and Sundays.

Upon reaching my six months at the shelter, I was instructed to write a letter to a government program explaining my current situation. I was told to be honest with them on how the programs at the center helped me to become independent and self-sufficient. After writing the letter, I received a response from the agency in no time that I was approved to move into one of the apartments they had. I was going to be reunited with Aaron.

Moving day came, I had all of my belongings packed and the lead team member gave me the instructions on how the day was going to proceed. She said that I was going to be taken to the apartment and another member would pick up Aaron and bring him to me at the new apartment. We were going to be living in this place for one year. I know to some that this might have not seemed like a long time or a big deal, but to me it was the greatest news and seemed like forever. I was loaded into a van and taken to my new place. They wanted to surprise me, so I was blind folded. When we arrived and the blind fold came off, I could barely hold my excitement. When I was approved to move, they asked me where my favorite place was to go. I told them church. They had decorated the apartment in spiritual quotes and scriptures. There was a beautiful wreath hanging on the front door. Despite the strict rules that I still had to abide by, I was so glad to be in my own place.

Being in this new place made me feel more independent than ever. While residing in this place, I heard the Lord speak to me and tell me to go back to school and get my high school diploma. I adhered to the programs and attended my weekly classes. I learned life skills, budgeting, and how not to become a victim again. Aaron and I both enjoyed staying here. The year came and went quicker than I thought it would. The program was set up in a manner that when I paid a portion of my rent, I was putting money towards my down payment for when I moved. I was also able to find a new apartment quickly. It was hard to say good-bye to my advocate, but she ensured that I was ready to stand on my own.

God blessed me even the more. I met my now current Godfearing husband. God led me to become a member of an apostolic church. I went to revival one night and there was a gentleman sitting in front of me. There was something about him. I couldn't see his face, but from his profile he was handsome. After my pastor was done preaching, he told us to shake our neighbors' hands. I couldn't wait to stick my hand out to shake the man's hand in front of me.

I never thought I would ever see this man again. The next day I had to go to the grocery store. I started not to go, but I changed my mind and processed to go to the store. As I got closer to the meat counter, I saw the man from the revival. It was like I had lost something and found it. He spotted me and we exchanged pleasantries. As I walked up and down each aisle, I kept my eye on him until he left out of the store. Again, I thought that I would never see this man again; my heart dropped. Less than a week later, I seen him at the wake of my Bishop. After exchanging pleasantries this time, he didn't walk away. Instead he asked me for my phone number.

As we got to know each other over time, I found out that he was related the pastor's wife of the little church on Dickson Street. He also revealed to me that the night of the revival when the pastor told the congregation to shake your neighbor's hand, he felt that I was going to be his wife. He began to tell me that he saw a light around me, and he was so focused on me that he didn't see anyone else. Our meeting was destined by God. He informed me that his cousin brought him to the revival and sat in the back of the church, so no one thought that they were a couple. She also brought him to the store that was near my apartment instead of his house. God ordained for us to be together and I am so grateful the love of my life. I am now in college studying to become a social worker. It is my desire to reach out to touch as many lives as I can. I want to teach people how to love themselves knowing that God love them too. God is The Light That Brought Me Through. He can bring you through as well.

www.ingramcontent.com/pod-product-compliance
Lightning Source LLC
Chambersburg PA
CBHW071714040426
42446CB00011B/2060